Simple Rhythms

Poetry for Runners

Ray Charbonneau

Copyright 2017 by Ray Charbonneau

First Edition

ISBN: 978-1544011790

Also by Ray Charbonneau:
Chasing the Runner's High
R is for Running
Overthinking the Marathon
Idle Feet Do the Devil's Work
The 27th Mile (editor)
More info:
http://www.y42k.com/books/

Book Design: Y42K Publishing Services
http://www.y42k.com/publishing-services/

*For race directors,
everyone who has ever volunteered to help at a race,
and everyone who's helped put on a group run.*

And as always, for Ruth

Table of Contents

Foreword 7
Simple Rhythms 9
Staying Afloat 11
Same Old Song 13
Interlude #1 15
The Runner 17
Product Placement 21
Einstein Was a Runner 25
Interlude #2 27
Run Like the Dickens 29
Elemental 33
It's Running Season 35
Coda 37
About the Author 39
Credits 40

Foreword

Running is a simple and basic activity. One foot in front of the other, pounding out a rhythmic beat in 2/4 time. Often, traditional Western poetry also consists of feet laid out one after another. Coincidence? I think not.

Poetry isn't always as simple as running, but running does give you time to think, and anything that you do regularly can take on layers of meaning. It was Shakespeare that wrote, "Bid me run, and I will strive with things impossible."

Of course, I'm no Shakespeare. Even so, I hope you find this collection to be worth lingering over, like a long, slow run with friends.

Thanks for reading,
Ray

"Running track and cross-country turned out to be important to my life. Training hard, not quitting even when you were dead tired, gave me a discipline that has stayed with me for the rest of my life."

-Senator Bernie Sanders

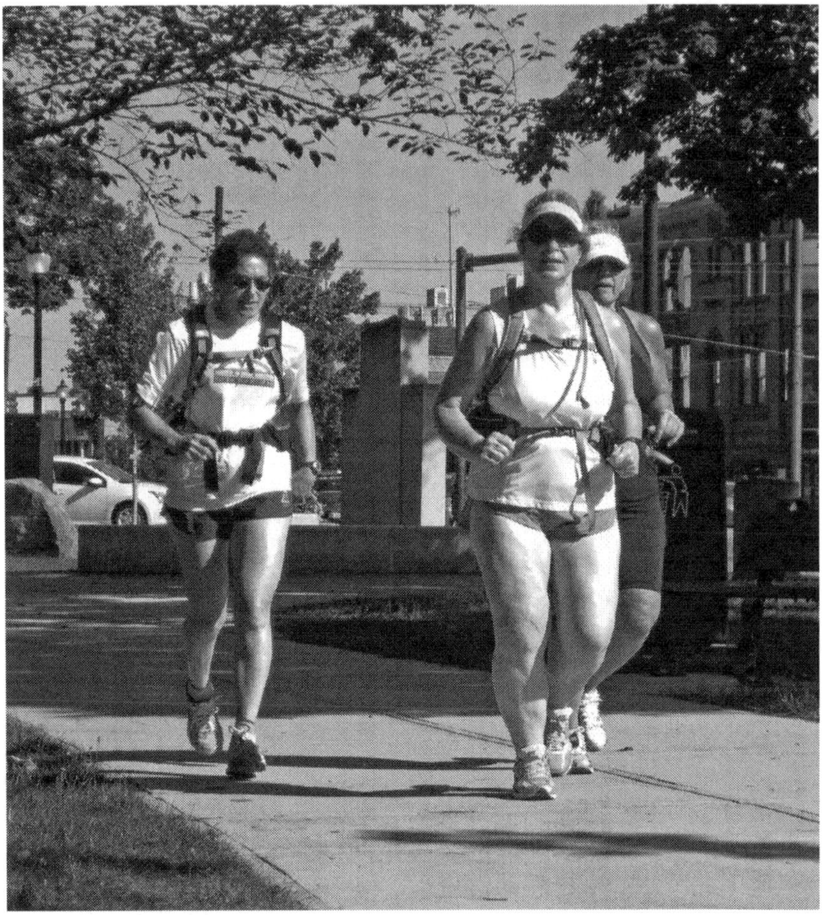

Simple Rhythms

I run for ease, I run thru pain
I run for health, and to stay thin
It clears the noise out from my brain
It helps me test the shape I'm in
I run alone, I run in groups
On all terrains, in all the weathers
Sometimes on tracks in endless loops
If I could I'd run forever
I run on rocks, I run through slop
I run from angst, in search of calm
Maybe go on when I should stop
Each step defines the path I'm on
I run from need, I run to be
I run to make the best of me

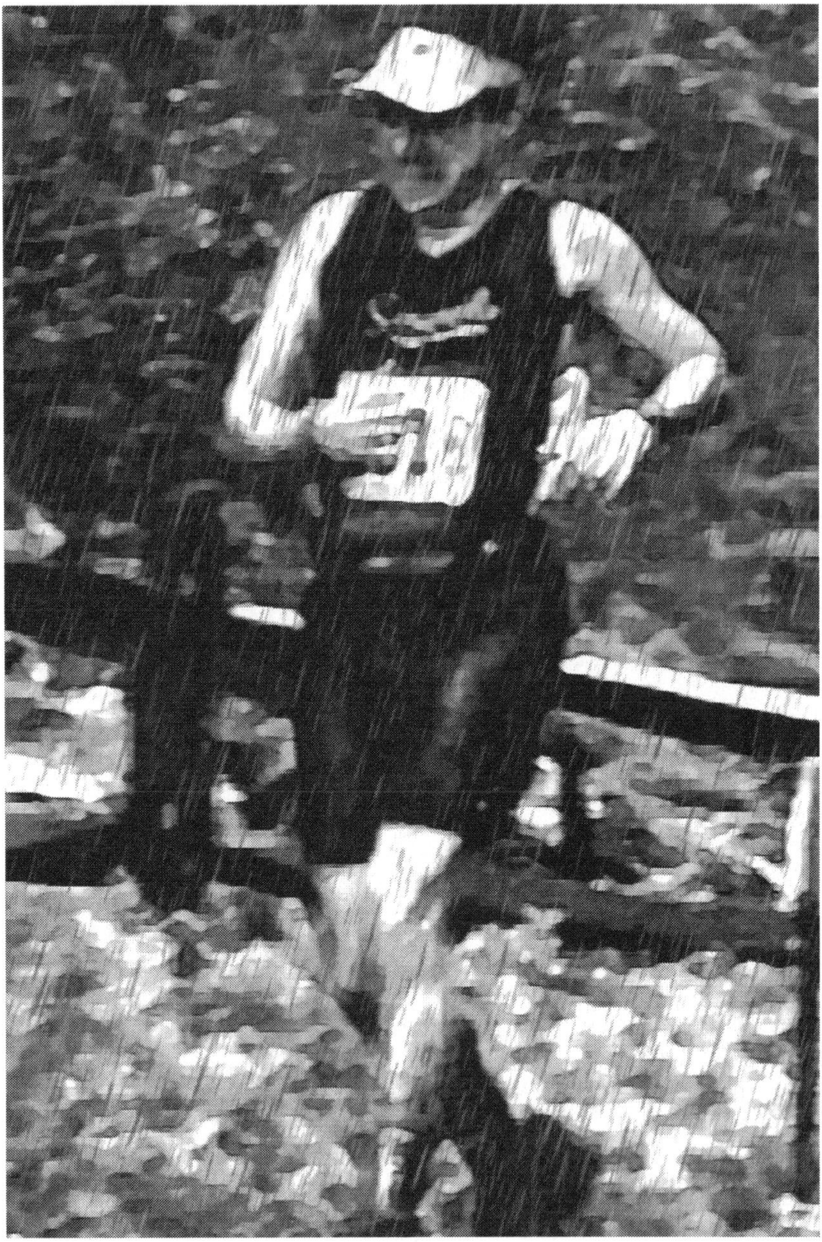

Staying Afloat

I once planned every run weeks in advance,
Crafting a mix of speed, distance, and terrain
Asking whether each run was the best I could do
To arrive at the start ready to unleash
A torrent of strides, flowing over the course
Storming the finish as rapidly as I could.
But each of those steps was one more drop
Slowly eroding rapids to streams.
Now that my intervals are more often walk breaks
I think as little as possible; avoid asking 'whether?'
Just check the weather and head out the door
Feet pit-pattering a gentle shower
As I hope to get six miles from home
Before I decide that ten is enough.
I no longer finish as fast as I used to
What's important is that the running never ends.

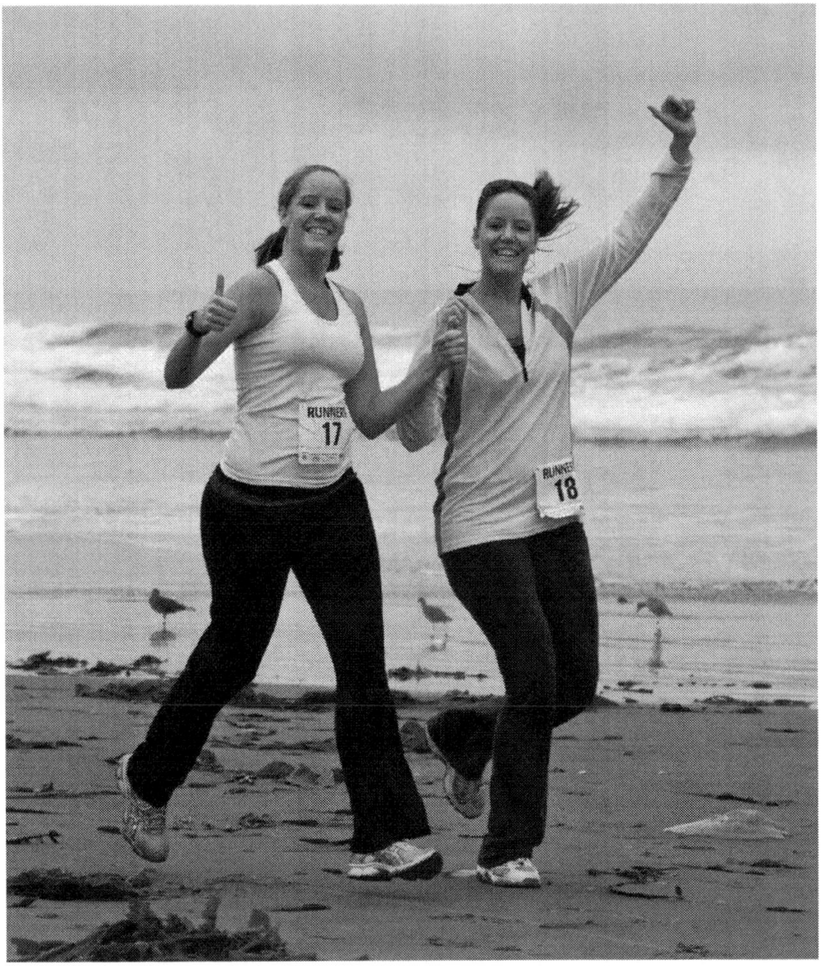
17
18

Same Old Song

Running is boring, so some people say
One step, then another, grim day after day.
That repetition is not cause for alarm.
A litany of footfalls is part of the charm
Of the music I hear on the roads and the trails
And out on the paths where there used to be rails.
The beat of my feet pounding regular rhythm
Reliably backs up the day's lyricism.
Like the stark, somber chant of a grey winter sky,
Or the light, happy tunes of the birds as they fly.
Today's run is sonorous, a song long and slow.
Tomorrow it's time to increase the tempo.
Sprint, rest, and repeat, or a little fartlek.
Perfect intervals are a worthy target.
On days when my friends come along on my run,
A popular tune is a jog just for fun.
Sure, at times pain will play a sour note,
But the music is worth all the time I devote.

Interlude #1

Pragmatically shod
Canter 'round the track each day
Eat like a horse, too.

Light shoes and right fit
Happy feet make spirit soar
Help body to fly

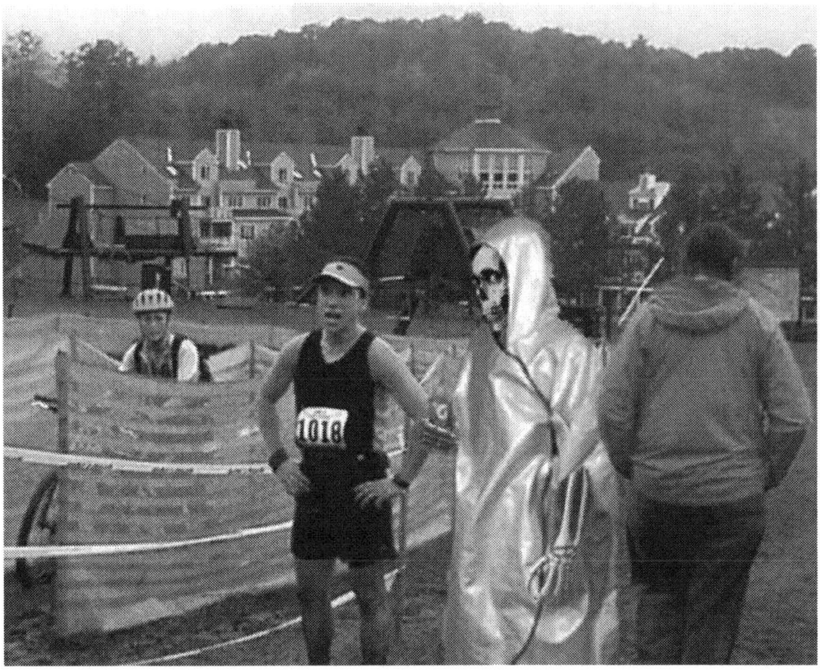
1018

The Runner

(with apologies to E. A. Poe)

Once upon a hillside dreary, a man pondered, weak and weary
Fifty miles had left him teary, pain that he could not ignore
As the sweat dripped, nearly blinding, and the blisters kept on grinding
He made a choice that was binding, finding that he'd run no more.
"This's the last one," said the runner, grateful that he'd run no more
"Damn, my knees are really sore."

After running fifty miles, even death would give him smiles
If it meant that running's trials - pain and boredom - were done for
Over the thunderous beating of his heart he stood, repeating
"I no longer am competing. It stops here," he truly swore
"I am really done competing," once again he truly

swore
"Running stops forever more."

For all his life he kept that oath, to run one more step he was loath
His stomach showed a rapid growth, a tighter belt that he deplored
On the couch he faced each morrow, in larger clothes he had to borrow
Hiding in the fear of sorrow—sorrow from pain he abhored
When asked if he would run again, mindful of what he abhored
Quoth the runner; "Nevermore."

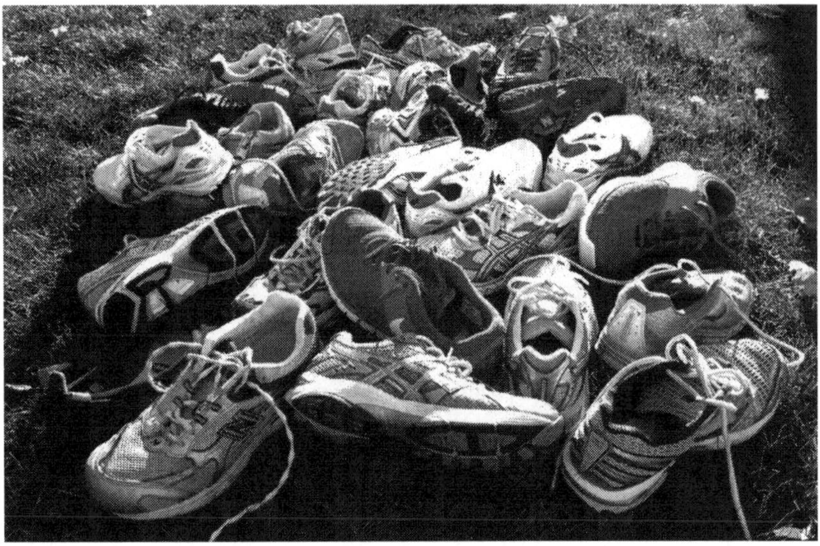

Product Placement

The hunt for the right running shoe
Is bound to make you come unglued.
Searching for just the perfect sole
Can cost a lot, and takes a toll.
So many brands. What should you do
To find the shoe that's right for you?

Run on the roads in Air from Nike.
Or Zoom in flats or their shoes spiky.
Though if you want to run like Meb
Buy Skechers 'cause he's their celeb.
Are FreshFoam soles made by New Balance
The ones you need to hone your talents?
A cushy pad of ASICS Gel
Can make it so your feet don't swell.
The Brooks' midsoles with DNA.
Mold to your stride, or so they say.
Rather run in La Sportiva
With LaSpEVA? I believe ya.
POWERGRID no longer fun?
Saucony switched to Everrun.
If loose shoes leave you in the dumps
Try Reeboks with their built-in pumps.

Some Puma runners ask "Why knot?"
And twist the Disc to keep shoes taut.
If theirs are on the narrow side,
These Topos run a little wide.
Trail runners? Accelerate
In Meta-Shanks from INOV-8.
Never trip nor fall on your face
With Salomons snugly Speedlaced
North Face, Merrill, or Montrail?
Maybe one of those won't fail.
Minimalism's appeal lingers?
Vibram still sells their Five Fingers.
Like some padding with zero drop?
Make a trip to the Altra shop.
If I say 'cushion', you say 'more',
Then head down to the HOKA store.
Too much foam makes you a slug?
Try Newton's bouncy forefoot lugs.
Or if you want to run on springs
Enko and Spira have those things.
Mizounos let me ride the waves.
On's Cloudsurfers are not my faves.
Do you prefer Pearl Izumi?
Haven't tried 'em, please don't sue me.

Any shoes, even adidas
Can help avoid the dreaded big ass.
But hopefully this little guide
Was able to help you decide.
And if the perfect shoe you find
Buy lots, before they're redesigned.

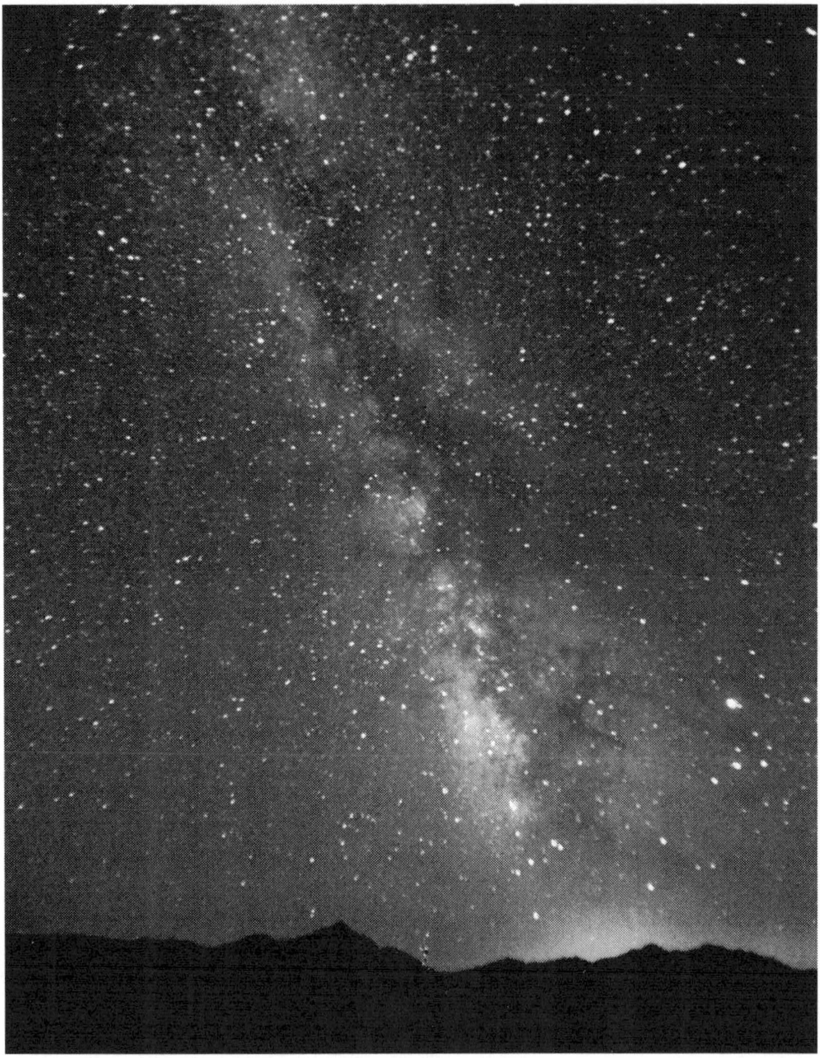

Einstein Was a Runner

At times when I'm running a marathon
It seems like the race will never end,
Crawling along at only 8 miles per hour,
When the winner has already split the tape.
But as Einstein taught us, everything is relative.
We're running a course on a rotating Earth
Whose surface circles its axis at 800 miles per hour
While the planet orbits our Sun at 66,600 miles per hour
As that star whirls around the Milky Way core at 483,000 miles per hour,
A galaxy that's moving through an ever-expanding universe at 1,300,000 miles per hour.
So when a race that once seemed like it might take an eternity
Or an eon, or a year, or at least a day
Ends less than two hours after the winner's,
Viewed from the right frame of reference
That's not bad.

Interlude #2

There once was a runner at Boston
Whose sense of direction did cost him
He was in first place
Near the end of the race
Went left on Hereford and we lost him

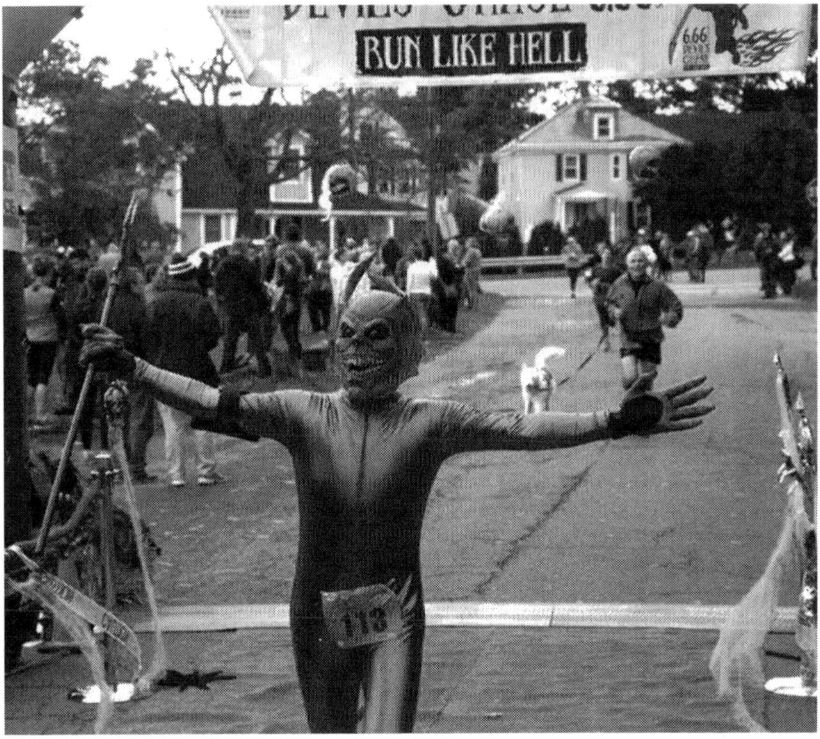
RUN LIKE HELL

Run Like the Dickens

They say that I run
Like I'm chased by the devil.
They think it's a compliment
And a metaphor.
Well, yes it is,
Just not how they think.
The demons aren't behind me
Out on the course.
They're waiting
Back at home
Back at work
Waiting for the run to end
Waiting for when I'm alone
Without the ritual of running
To shield me.
Running farther and faster,
Absorbing more punishment,
That's not the way
To exorcise my demons.
I'll run out of endurance
Before I run out of miles.
No matter how far I go
There is always more pain.

But casting a circle of salty sweat
Creates a cone of power
That wards off the demons
When the circle is closed.
A few torrid miles
Won't atone for my sins
But they give me the strength
To carry on.

Event
26.2
Rn
Symbol
Chemical Name
Runner
180
Strides/ Minute

Elemental

All the best runners are master alchemists
Adepts of using the Philosopher's Stone
To transmute base miles into gold
Metamorphosing as needed
To flow liquidly downhill, or
Ascend ethereally, wafting on the breezes
The rest of the time as solid as the ground they stride across
Until it's time to burn

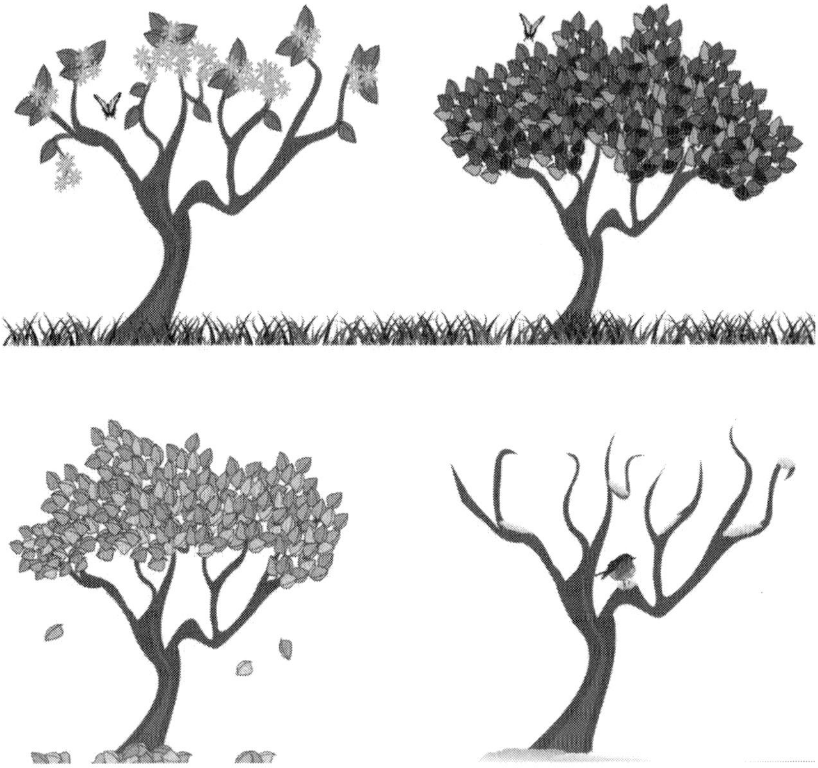

It's Running Season

Crunching through unbroken expanses of white
Under a sky sullen with the burden of even more snow
It's bitter cold, 2 below
We are thickclads
Layers of polypro and fleece
Replacing the fat not stored
During our fall harvest of miles
The only splashes of color
A fluorescent green jacket, a bright orange hat
Lacy with shining tendrils of frozen sweat
Comfort comes from effort
Our legs keep moving, and
Soon enough we're warm enough
The sun higher in the sky
The snow lower on the ground
Green buds and purple crocuses poking through
Bare arms and legs poking out
Planting one foot in front of the other
Sowing miles in endless roads
Weeding out weakness, plowing forward
Watering ourselves more heavily
Clothing reduced to the bare minimum
Lacy with crusty tendrils of dried sweat

As the heat reaches its zenith
Harsh colors muted by the shades
We peer through, searching for shade
Until thunder rumbles in the skies
The heat breaks, the sun drops and
We storm through falling leaves
Reaping what we've sown
In a whirlwind of orange and yellow and red
Then continuing on tired legs
Exhausting puffs of cold breath
Tracking our training in the cold
Through the 5 o'clock shadows
From the stubble of leafless trees
Dripping with a wintry mix
As we push the pace for warmth
Crunching through unbroken expanses of white

Coda

Running for yang, Running from yin
It gives my life some discipline
A post-race beer? No contradiction
The finish line is my addiction

About the Author

Ray Charbonneau is the author of a number of books on running. That number is currently five. He's also the editor of *The 27th Mile*, an anthology in memory of the victims of the Boston Marathon bombing.

Ray has run more than thirty marathons and ultramarathons, including one and a half 100 mile races, without winning a single one. But there's always tomorrow.

Ray lives in Arlington, Massachusetts, with his wife and their two cats. You can often find Ray and Ruth out on the streets running, but Felix and Phoebe stay inside.

Ray's articles on running have appeared in the Boston Globe, Marathon & Beyond, UltraRunning, Level Renner, Cool Running, and other publications.

If you have any comments, running stories you want to share, or know of a good way to dispose of used running shoes, you can contact Ray at writeray@y42k.com.

For more information, visit y42k.com.

Credits

Art:

Cover: art by Frank Pichel

Same Old Song: courtesy of Mike Baird under the Creative Commons Attribution 2.0 Generic license

Einstein Was a Runner: courtesy of Steve Jurvetson (as edited by Fountains of Bryn Mawr) under the Creative Commons Attribution 2.0 Generic license

Run Like the Dickens: by Jarek Lepak Photography, courtesy of B&S Event Management/2016 Devils Chase 6.66 Mile Road Race

Elemental: courtesy of Allison Lynch

It's Running Season: courtesy of Pascal Charneau under the Creative Commons Zero 1.0 Public Domain License via openclipart.com

All other art is from the author's collection.

For more information about Creative Commons licensing, visit:
https://creativecommons.org/

Some of the work in this book appeared previously in *Level Renner* magazine and at *Queen Mob's Teahouse*.

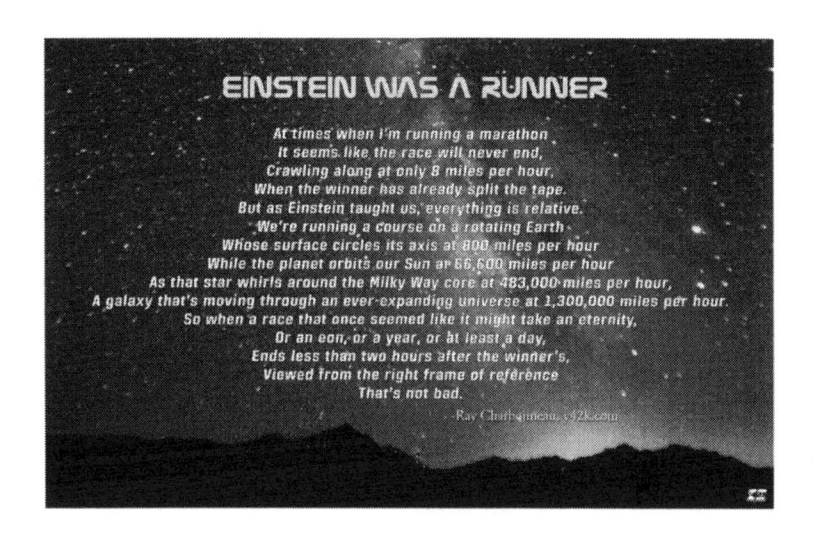

> **EINSTEIN WAS A RUNNER**
>
> At times when I'm running a marathon
> It seems like the race will never end,
> Crawling along at only 8 miles per hour,
> When the winner has already split the tape.
> But as Einstein taught us, everything is relative.
> We're running a course on a rotating Earth
> Whose surface circles its axis at 800 miles per hour
> While the planet orbits our Sun at 66,600 miles per hour
> As that star whirls around the Milky Way core at 483,000 miles per hour,
> A galaxy that's moving through an ever-expanding universe at 1,300,000 miles per hour.
> So when a race that once seemed like it might take an eternity,
> Or an eon, or a year, or at least a day,
> Ends less than two hours after the winner's,
> Viewed from the right frame of reference
> That's not bad.
>
> -Ray Charbonneau, y42k.com

Custom artwork inspired by the poem "Einstein Was a Runner" is available printed on high-quality poster paper with a matte finish. Other sizes, paper types, and framing options are available. You can also get the image printed on greeting cards, coffee cups, and numerous other items.

For more information, and to get yours:
http://www.y42k.com/posters/

Books by Ray Charbonneau
For more info:
http://www.y42k.com/books/

Pass the Baton! is a great game for runners and for anyone who likes a fast-paced strategy game. Two running clubs, the Red River Runners and the Blue Blazing Bolts, compete to win the Big Relay. Your goal as team captain is to manage your club's runners so they beat the other team and carry your baton across the finish line first!

Pass the Baton! is only $14.99. Order your copy at: http://www.y42k.com/games/

Interested in publishing your own book?

Y42K Publishing Services can help you design and publish your book quickly, professionally, and at a low cost. Unlike other services that automate the process, I'll work directly with you every step of the way to ensure you get the book you want.

For more information, visit the Y42K Publishing Services page at:

http://www.y42k.com/publishing-services/

Made in the USA
Middletown, DE
19 March 2017